GRAPHIC HISTORY

THE STORY OF THE STATUE OF LIBERTY

by Xavier Niz
illustrated by Cynthia Martin
and Brent Schoonover

Consultant:
Barbara Truesdell, PhD
Assistant Director
Center for the Study of History and Memory
Indiana University, Bloomington, Indiana

Capstone press
Mankato, Minnesota

Graphic Library is published by Capstone Press,
151 Good Counsel Drive, P.O. Box 669, Mankato, Minnesota 56002.
www.capstonepress.com

Printed in the United States of America

1 2 3 4 5 6 11 10 09 08 07 06

Library of Congress Cataloging-in-Publication Data
Niz, Xavier.
The story of the Statue of Liberty / by Xavier Niz; illustrated by Cynthia Martin and Brent Schoonover.
p. cm.—(Graphic library. Graphic history)
Summary: "In graphic novel format, tells the story of the building of the Statue of Liberty"—Provided by publisher.
Includes bibliographical references and index.
ISBN-13: 978-0-7368-5494-8 (hardcover)
ISBN-10: 0-7368-5494-0 (hardcover)
1. Statue of Liberty (New York, N.Y.)—Juvenile literature. 2. New York (N.Y.)—Buildings, structures, etc.—Juvenile literature. I. Martin, Cynthia, 1961– ill. II. Schoonover, Brent, ill. III. Title. IV. Series.
F128.64.L6N59 2006
974.7'1—dc22 2005028953

Art Direction and Design
Jason Knudson

Production Designer
Alison Thiele

Storyboard Artist
Alison Thiele

Colorist
Brent Schoonover

Editor
Christopher Harbo

Editor's note: Direct quotations from primary sources are indicated by a yellow background.

Direct quotations appear on the following pages:
Page 27, from *The Writings and Speeches of Grover Cleveland* by George F. Parker (New York: Kraus Reprint, 1970).

Table of Contents

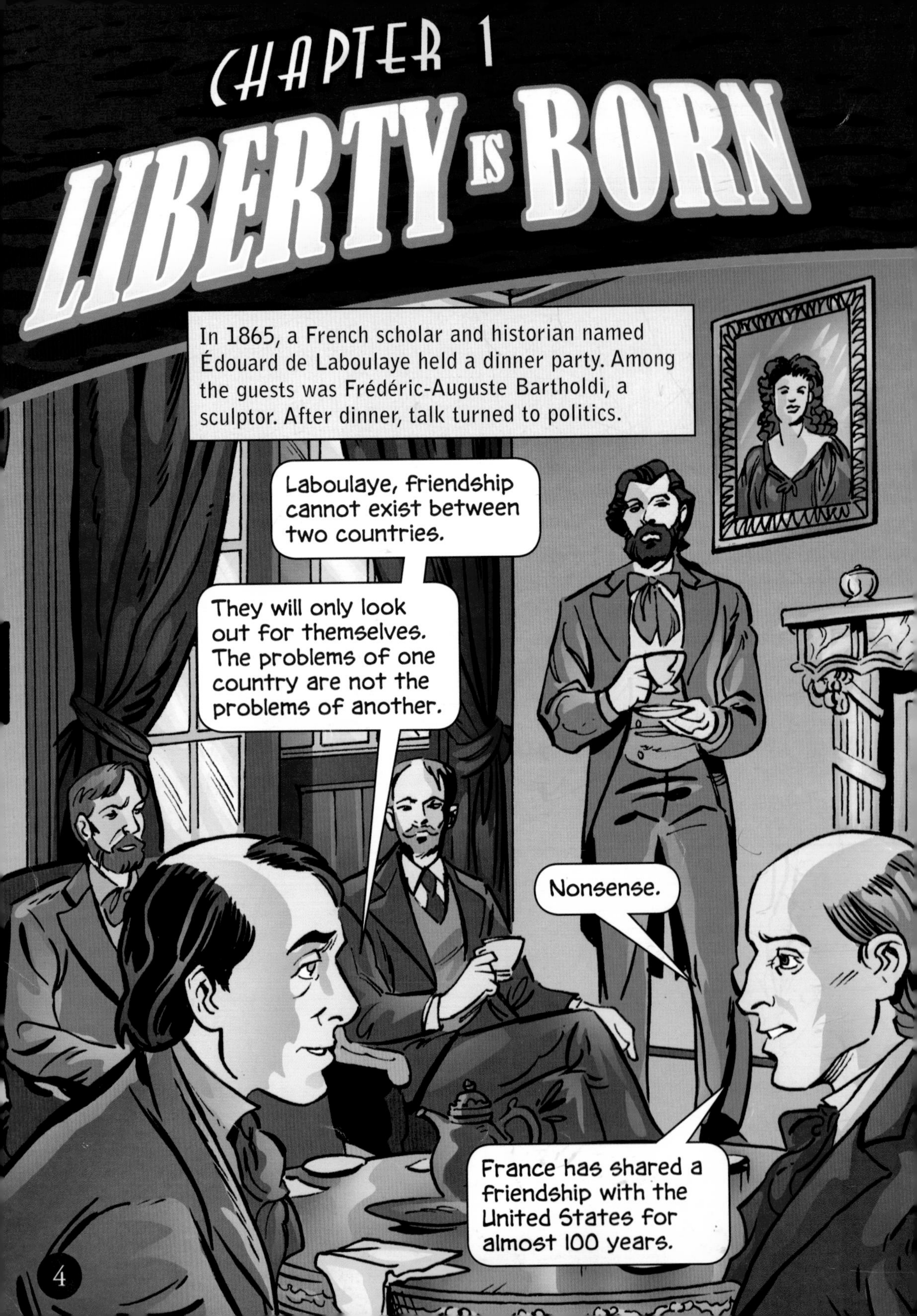
CHAPTER 1
LIBERTY IS BORN
In 1865, a French scholar and historian named Édouard de Laboulaye held a dinner party. Among the guests was Frédéric-Auguste Bartholdi, a sculptor. After dinner, talk turned to politics.
Laboulaye, friendship cannot exist between two countries.
They will only look out for themselves. The problems of one country are not the problems of another.
Nonsense.
France has shared a friendship with the United States for almost 100 years.

During the American Revolutionary War, France sent money and troops to help the American colonies fight the British.
In the United States, people respect French soldiers like Lafayette just as much as their own heroes.
Even today, our two nations believe in freedom and independence. We need a way to celebrate our shared beliefs.
Like a monument? Something to stand for our common bond?
Exactly, Bartholdi!

Seven years later, Laboulaye took the first step in making his idea a reality.
You have a job for me?
I want you to go to America. Study the country and the people.
See if they will help build a monument to the friendship between our countries.
Bartholdi arrived in New York Harbor on June 21, 1871.
Excuse me. Do you know the name of that island?
That's Bedloe's Island.
It is perfect for our monument. Every ship in the harbor passes it.

Bartholdi traveled across the United States. Everywhere he went, he took notes about what he saw.
Chicago, Illinois
Salt Lake City, Utah
San Francisco, California
With letters of introduction from Laboulaye, Bartholdi met many important people.
President Grant, it's an honor to meet you.
I look forward to seeing this monument you are planning.

Upon returning to Paris, Bartholdi began sketching ideas for the monument.
Everything in America is so big. Only a truly colossal monument will work.
Libertas. The Roman goddess of freedom. Perfect!
At that time, Libertas appeared on the seal of the French Republic and on American money.

Bartholdi worked on his design for the next four years.
The crown is perfect!
But the left hand needs more work.
Finally in 1875, Bartholdi showed Laboulaye his final design.
I present you with—
—Liberty Enlightening the World!
Wonderful! How tall will she stand?
150 feet!

CHAPTER 2
LIBERTY TAKES SHAPE
On November 6th, 1875, Bartholdi's final design was revealed at a fund-raising banquet at the Hotel du Louvre in Paris.
She will be a symbol of the friendship between the people of the United States and the people of France.
Our government shouldn't pay for this statue.
Don't worry. Laboulaye started the Franco-American Union.
It will collect money from ordinary citizens to build the statue.
Laboulaye raised enough money to begin building the statue. He hoped to have it built by the following summer. The United States would be celebrating 100 years of independence from Britain.

This is a huge project. Can you handle the job?
We are ready for the challenge!
Bartholdi built several models of the statue before construction began. The largest was 36 feet tall. Workers placed a great number of small dots on this model.
It's time to take that one apart so we can start on the full-sized pieces.
The 36-foot model was split into several smaller pieces. Then, the distance between the dots on each piece was measured and multiplied by four. This gave the dimensions for the completed version of each piece.

Then workers built each section of the full-scale statue.
Hurry up now boys! We need to finish putting the plaster on the model.
Easy now. Lift it carefully.
When the plaster dried, the workers built molds with strips of wood. The molds followed the shape of the plaster.

Sheets of copper were then placed into the molds and hammered into shape.
The pieces of copper were welded together to form the skin of the statue.
There's just no way we can finish the statue by July 4.
How about just the right hand and the torch? I'd like to have something to present to the Americans.
We've got 20 men working 10 hours a day, seven days a week. We'll do our best.

By May 1876, Bartholdi left for the American Centennial. In September, the right hand and torch were unveiled at the Centennial celebration in Philadelphia.
It's truly impressive!
Just imagine what the finished statue will look like!

Bartholdi went to New York after unveiling the torch. He needed to start fund-raising to pay for the statue's pedestal.
The American branch of the Franco-American Union should pay for the statue's pedestal. Will you be able to raise enough money?
The statue is popular with the people right now. Raising money shouldn't be a problem.
Have you seen the papers?!
I don't believe this!
The New York Times says that the statue will cost $2 million. And that New Yorkers will have to pay for it.
But that's not true!

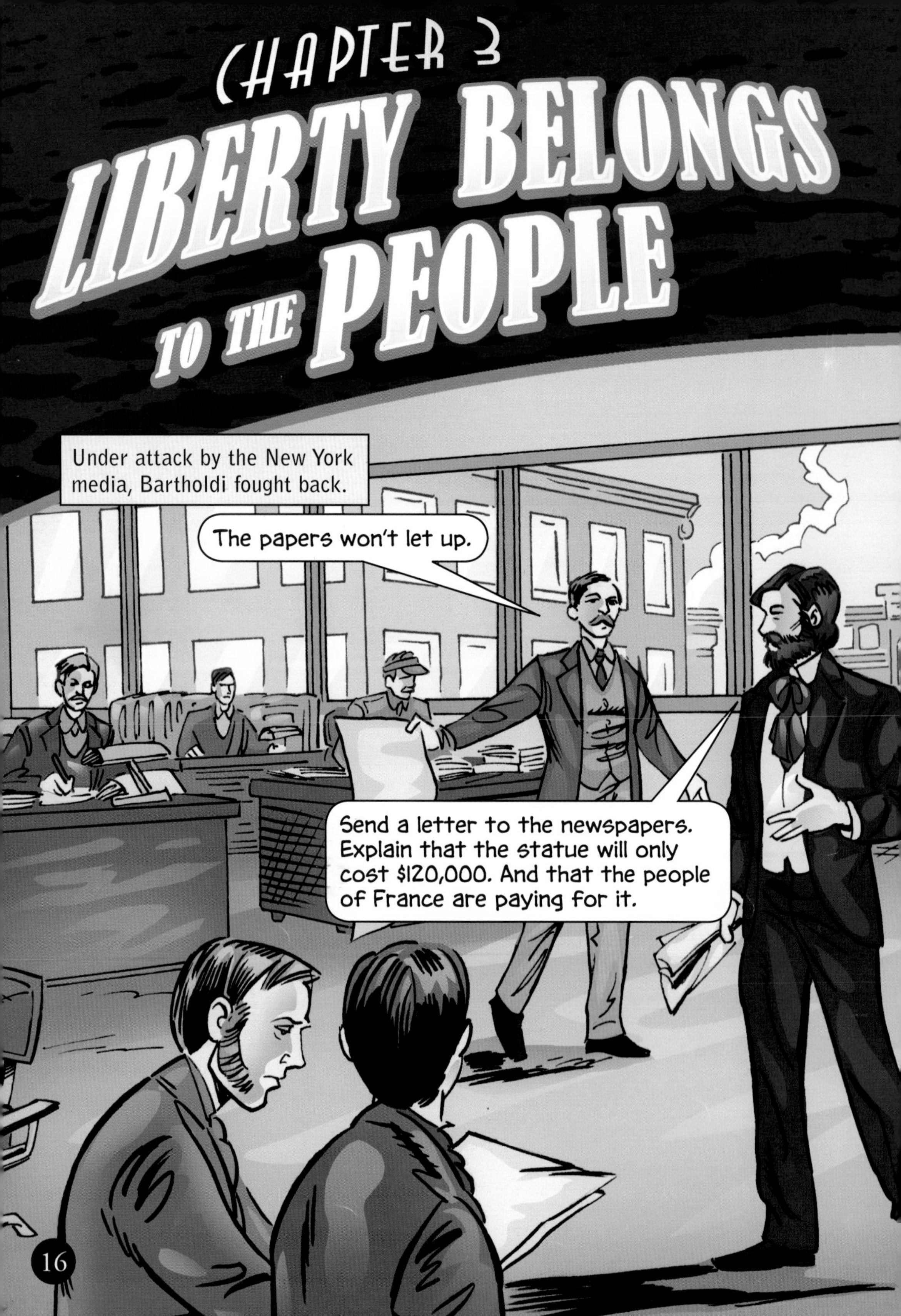
CHAPTER 3
LIBERTY BELONGS TO THE PEOPLE
Under attack by the New York media, Bartholdi fought back.
The papers won't let up.
Send a letter to the newspapers. Explain that the statue will only cost $120,000. And that the people of France are paying for it.

Now the papers are saying that if New York doesn't want the statue, Philadelphia or Boston will pay for it.
Send them all letters. We must stop these shameful lies. My statue will be built on Bedloe's Island.
Bartholdi's efforts started to pay off. On February 22, 1877, the House of Representatives met to discuss a resolution concerning the statue.
Since there are no objections, we accept the statue as a gift from the people of France.
Furthermore, we authorize Bedloe's Island to be offered as the site for the statue.
On February 27, the Senate passed the same resolution. A few days later, President Grant signed it into law.

With his success in America, Bartholdi returned home to work on the statue.
Laboulaye! What's wrong?
Terrible news!
We've spent most of our money and the public is losing interest. I don't know how we will raise more to finish the statue.
What about next year's Universal Exposition in Paris? Perhaps we can unveil another piece of the statue there?
Amazing!

When most of the outer skin was complete, Bartholdi turned to Alexandre-Gustave Eiffel, a famous French engineer.
My statue will be heavy. Can you find a way to keep it standing?
I am not worried. We will build a frame to support your statue from the inside.
Look at how the pieces fit together!
It will tower over all of Paris!
Eiffel designed a steel structure strong enough to support the statue's weight. He began with a large steel pylon in the center of the statue. Smaller steel girders extended out from the main pylon and attached to the copper skin.

Have you heard the good news?
We've raised enough money to finish the statue.
Even school children donated money.
This will truly be a gift from all the people of France.

Meanwhile, fund-raising for the pedestal started out well in America. By the fall of 1883, enough money had been raised to begin construction.
Once we get the foundation laid, we can start building the pedestal.
Easier said than done.
We're using 200 barrels of concrete a day. At this rate we won't be done until the spring.
The foundation was completed on May 17, 1884. By this time, work on the statue in Paris was almost completed. But Bartholdi had to wait to ship the statue to the United States. The Franco-American Union was having a hard time raising money to build the pedestal.
What do you mean we're running out of money? I thought we were doing fine.
We were. But the foundation alone cost twice our budget. If we don't raise more money soon, we'll have to stop work on the pedestal.

Despite its best efforts, the Union couldn't raise more money. Construction of the pedestal stopped in August 1884. At the New York newspaper the *World*, publisher Joseph Pulitzer was furious.
This is a national disgrace!
The French have finished the statue, yet we can't raise enough money to finish the pedestal?
What do you expect us to do about it, Mr. Pulitzer?
We will ask our readers for money. And we will publish the names of every person who donates.
Did you read this?
Yeah. I've got 50 cents in my pocket. I'll send it to them just to see my name in the paper.

Pulitzer's plan worked. In the first month of the campaign, the *World* raised more than $25,000.
Mr. Pulitzer! A 10-year-old boy donated 10 cents.
A young immigrant has enclosed his last two dollars.
Print the names of every last one of them!
Well, that's it! We've raised the $100,000 needed to complete the pedestal.
More than 120,000 people contributed to the fund.
This is truly the generosity of ordinary Americans.
With Pulitzer's campaign a success, construction of the pedestal resumed.

CHAPTER 4
LIBERTY COMES HOME

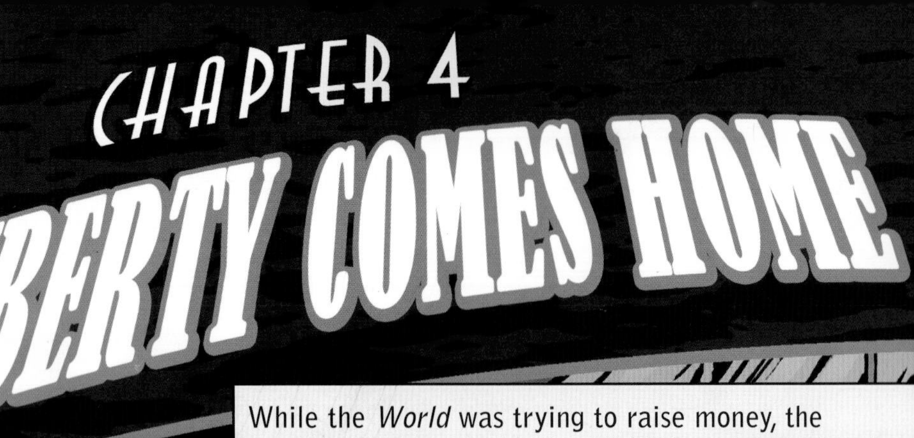

While the *World* was trying to raise money, the completed statue had been on display to the public in France. Finally, in January 1885, the statue was taken apart. Each piece was numbered and packed away.

How many crates do you think it will take?
According to my list, she should fit into 214 crates.

On May 21, 1885, the statue set out for America by ship.

Load those crates carefully.

On June 17, the statue arrived in New York Harbor. The crates were unpacked and the statue was stored until the pedestal was completed.
Finally, in April 1886, reconstruction of the statue began on Bedloe's Island. Piece by piece, the statue was put together on its new home.

On October 25, 1886, Bartholdi returned to New York for the unveiling of the statue. Upon his arrival, he was given a private tour of the statue.
So what do you think, Mr. Bartholdi?
Beautiful! She is truly a symbol of unity and friendship between two great nations.
The Statue of Liberty was officially unveiled on October 28, 1886. The day began with a parade down Fifth Avenue.
Isn't this fantastic?! Thousands of people have turned out.
It is indeed a wonderful sight, President Cleveland.

Later in the day, Bartholdi unveiled the face of his statue.
The day ended with a speech by President Cleveland, 21 years after the idea was first born.
We will not forget that Liberty has here made her home, nor shall her chosen altar be neglected.
In the years that followed, the statue was seen by millions of immigrants who passed through New York Harbor. For all those people, the statue stood for a chance to start a new life. The statue still stands as a symbol of freedom and independence.

MORE ABOUT THE STATUE OF LIBERTY

- Édouard de Laboulaye never lived to see his dream come true. He died on May 25, 1884, just two months before the statue was completed in France.
- The Statue of Liberty stands within the star-shaped walls of Fort Wood. Built from 1808 to 1811, Fort Wood protected part of New York Harbor for about 50 years.
- The pedestal was designed by American architect Richard Morris Hunt. Made of granite and concrete, the pedestal stands 154 feet high. When completed, its foundation was the world's largest concrete structure.
- At the time of its dedication, the Statue of Liberty was the tallest structure in New York City. Standing 305 feet (93 meters) tall, the statue remained the tallest structure until 1899 when the St. Paul's Building was built to 310 feet (94.5 meters).
- Some people believe the face of the Statue of Liberty is modeled after Frédéric-Auguste Bartholdi's mother.

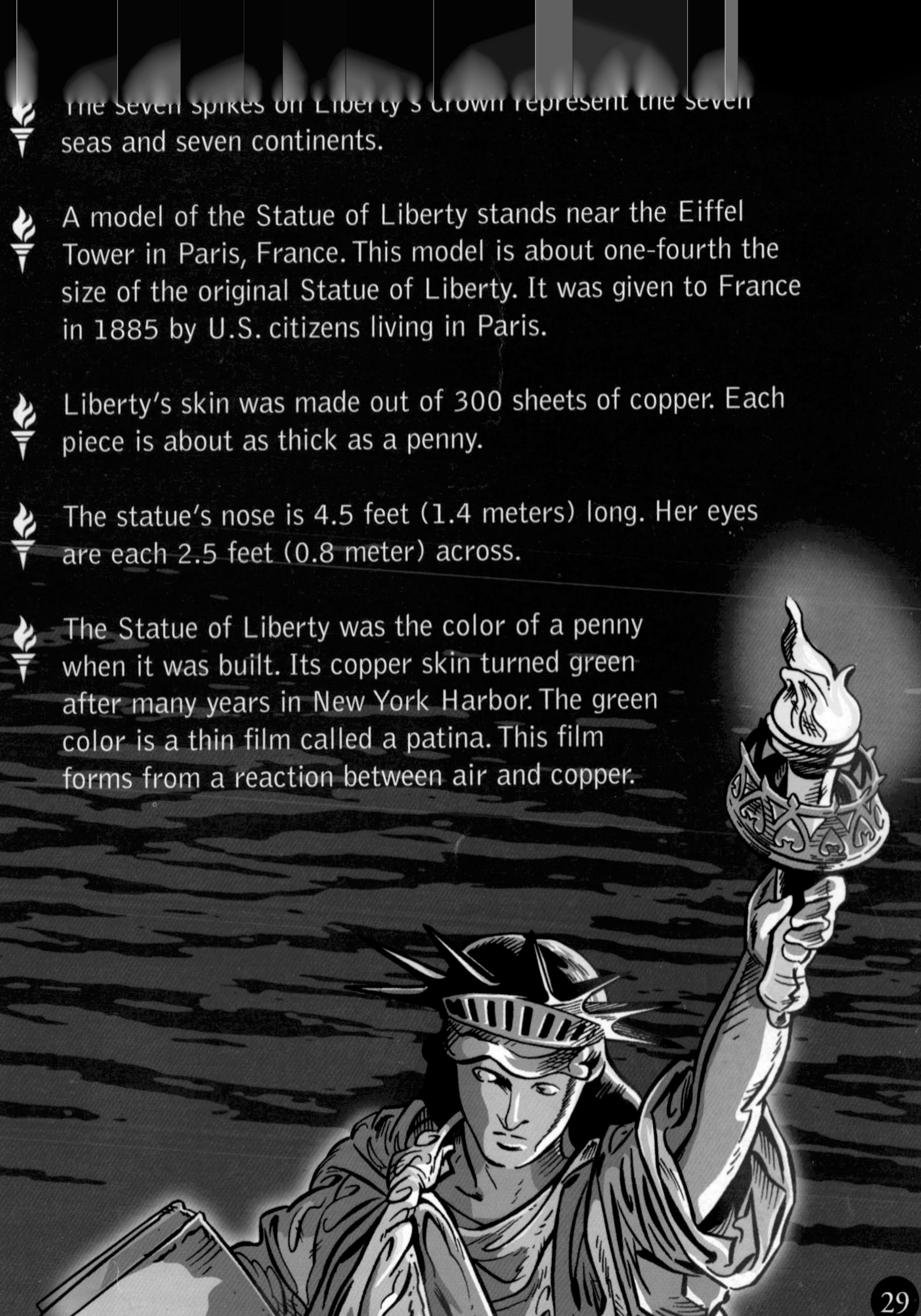

The seven spikes on Liberty's crown represent the seven seas and seven continents.

A model of the Statue of Liberty stands near the Eiffel Tower in Paris, France. This model is about one-fourth the size of the original Statue of Liberty. It was given to France in 1885 by U.S. citizens living in Paris.

Liberty's skin was made out of 300 sheets of copper. Each piece is about as thick as a penny.

The statue's nose is 4.5 feet (1.4 meters) long. Her eyes are each 2.5 feet (0.8 meter) across.

The Statue of Liberty was the color of a penny when it was built. Its copper skin turned green after many years in New York Harbor. The green color is a thin film called a patina. This film forms from a reaction between air and copper.

Glossary

campaign (kam-PAYN)—a series of actions organized over a period of time in order to achieve something

pedestal (PED-es-tuhl)—the bottom support of a statue or pillar

pylon (PYE-lon)—a tall, metal tower that supports a building or structure.

resolution (rez-uh-LOO-shuhn)—a formal statement of a decision

scholar (SKOL-ur)—a person who has done advanced study in a special field

Internet Sites

FactHound offers a safe, fun way to find Internet sites related to this book. All of the sites on FactHound have been researched by our staff.

Here's how:

1. *Visit www.facthound.com*
2. Type in this special code **0736854940** for age-appropriate sites. Or enter a search word related to this book for a more general search.
3. Click on the **Fetch It** button.

FactHound will fetch the best sites for you!

Read More

Ashley, Susan. *The Statue of Liberty.* Places in American History. Milwaukee: Weekly Reader Early Learning Library, 2004.

Hochain, Serge. *Building Liberty: A Statue Is Born.* Washington, D.C.: National Geographic, 2004.

Nobleman, Marc Tyler. *The Statue of Liberty.* First Facts. American Symbols. Mankato, Minn.: Capstone Press, 2003.

Whitelaw, Nancy. *Joseph Pulitzer and the New York World.* Makers of the Media. Greensboro, N.C.: Morgan Reynolds, 2000.

Bibliography

Bell, James B., and Richard I. Abrams. *In Search of Liberty: The Story of the Statue of Liberty and Ellis Island.* Garden City, N.Y.: Doubleday, 1984.

Handlin, Oscar, and the editors of the Newsweek Book Division. *Statue of Liberty.* Wonders of Man. New York: Newsweek, 1971.

Moreno, Barry. *The Statue of Liberty Encyclopedia.* New York: Simon & Schuster, 2000.

Parker, George F. *The Writings and Speeches of Grover Cleveland.* New York: Kraus Reprint, 1970.

INDEX